SEASONS

WINTER

Stephanie Turnbull

An Appleseed Editions book

Paperback edition 2015

First published in 2014 by Franklin Watts
338 Euston Road, London NW1 3BH

© 2012 Appleseed Editions

Created by Appleseed Editions Ltd,
Well House, Friars Hill, Guestling,
East Sussex TN35 4ET

Designed by Hel James
Edited by Mary-Jane Wilkins

A CIP record for this book is available from the British Library

ISBN 978 1 4451 3169 6

Dewey Classification: 508.2

Photo acknowledgements
t = top, b = bottom
page 1 karen roach/Shutterstock; 3 iStockphoto/
Thinkstock; 5 Alinute Silzeviciute/Shutterstock;
6 Pukhov Konstantin/Shutterstock; 7 Govorov Pavel/
Shutterstock; 8 iStockphoto/Thinkstock; 9 Zurijeta/
Shutterstock; 11 iStockphoto/Thinkstock;
12 iStockphoto/Thinkstock; 13 Douglas Freer/
Shutterstock; 14 iStockphoto/Thinkstock;
15 Al Mueller/Shutterstock; 16t Tony Campbell/
Shutterstock, b Jupiterimages/Thinkstock;
17 visceralimage/Shutterstock; 18 Zolran/
Shutterstock; 19 Couperfield/Shutterstock;
20 Jupiterimages/Thinkstock; 21 pio3/Shutterstock;
22 Anest/Shutterstock; 21 Digital Vision/Thinkstock,
hearts Dalibor Sevaljevic/Shutterstock
Cover Hemera/Thinkstock

Printed in China

Franklin Watts is a division of Hachette Children's Books, an Hachette UK company
www.hachette.co.uk

Contents

It's winter!

A hungry deer sniffs the frozen air.

Brrrr!

Our winter months are December, January and February.

The sun rises late every morning and sets early every evening. Days feel short and chilly.

Wear layers of warm clothes in winter. Don't forget a hat!

Ice everywhere

On very cold winter days, water freezes into ice. Long icicles hang from buildings.

In some countries, people skate and play hockey on lakes and rivers that have frozen solid.

White world

Sometimes water droplets in the air freeze together to make snowflakes. Softly they f
l
u
t
t
e
r

to the ground.

New snow sparkles in the sun. It crunches and squeaks as you plod through it.

Wild weather

Winter can be stormy. Strong winds and heavy snow make swirling blizzards.

Sometimes rain or hailstones hammer down.

Lots of snow may block roads. Snow ploughs work hard to clear them.

Take a break

Many trees and plants
stop growing in winter.

They look dead, but under the ground their roots are alive.
A blanket of snow protects them.

A few plants have winter berries or even flowers.

Hungry animals

Winter is a tough time for animals. There is less food to eat and water may be frozen.

Help birds survive the winter by giving them nuts, seeds and water.

Keeping warm

Birds fluff up their feathers to stay warm.

Some animals grow thicker fur. This Arctic fox has brown fur in summer…

…and thick, white fur in winter. Now it can hide in snow!

Cosy homes

Many animals make snug winter dens under the snow and curl up inside.

Some creatures go into a deep sleep.

These bats are sleeping in a cave.

A ferret pops up
from its den
to look
for food.

Winter fun

There is lots to do in winter. Many people celebrate Christmas, then the start of a new year.

Enjoy winter by sledging, spotting animals or snuggling up indoors with a book!

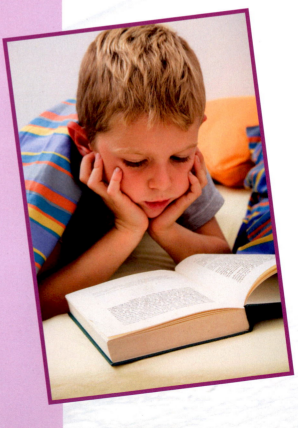

Did you know...?

When we have winter,
it is summer in the
southern half of
the world.

Every snowflake
has six points made
of tiny ice crystals.

Wood frogs freeze
solid in winter
and melt in spring.

Valentine's Day is on 14
February, when you send
cards to people you love!

Useful words

blizzard
A big snowstorm
with strong winds.

den
A hole or nest where
animals shelter and hide.

hailstone
A tiny ball of frozen rain.

winter
The time of year, called
a season, after autumn
and before spring.

Index